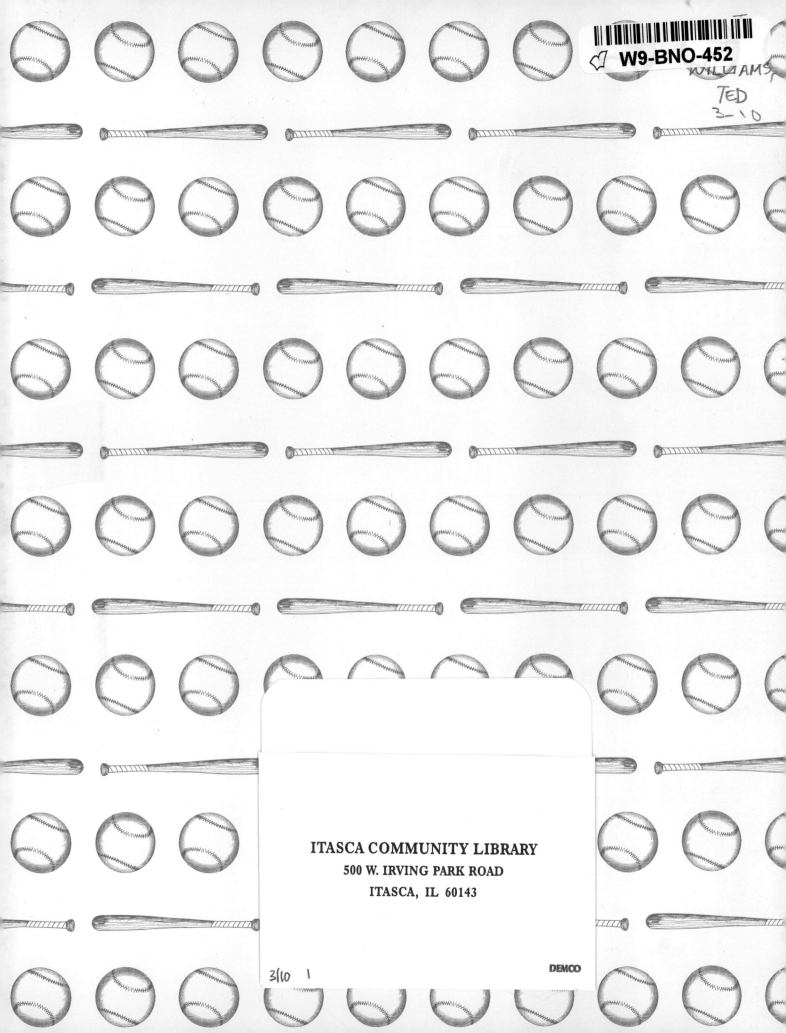

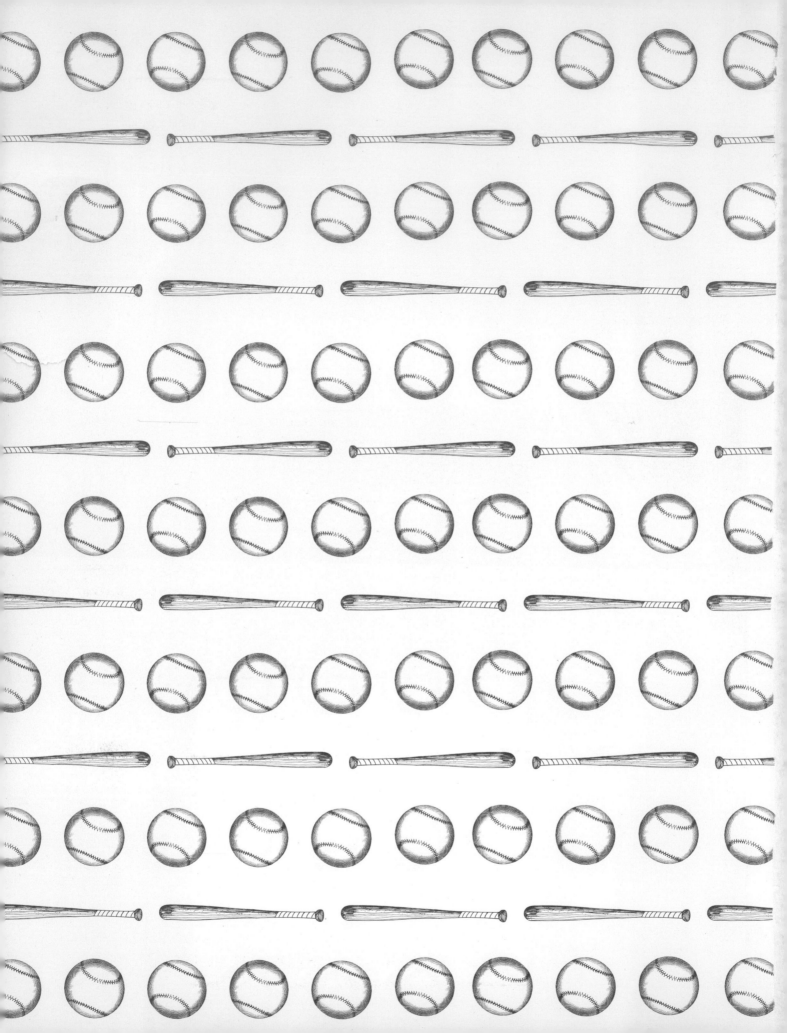

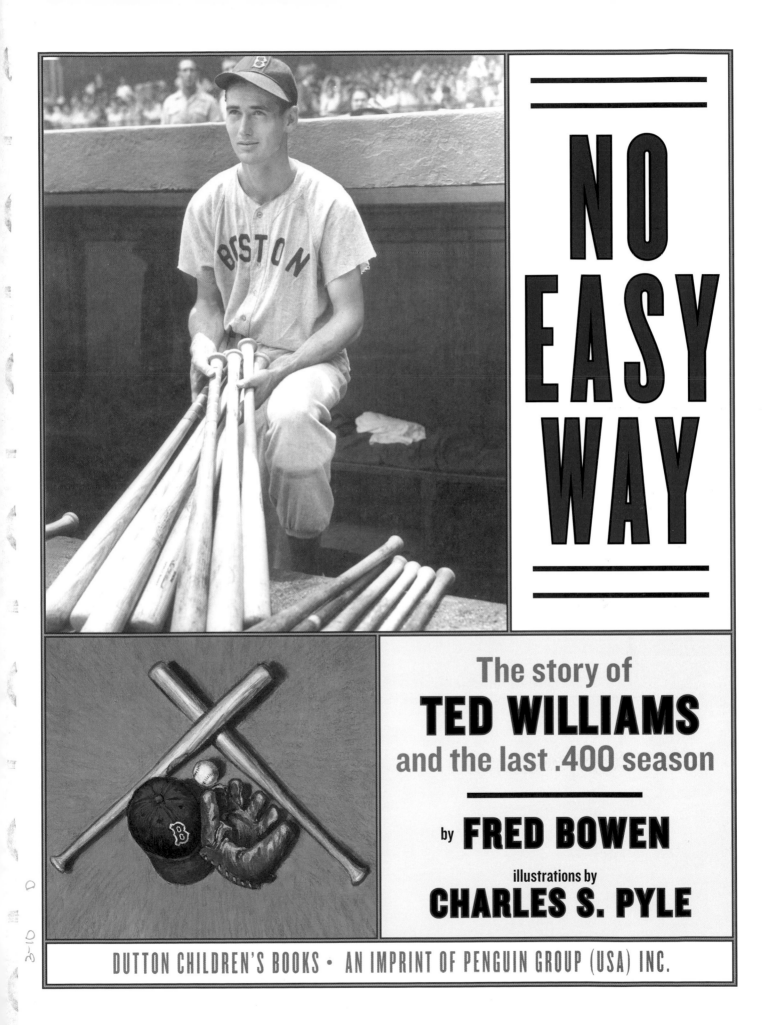

NO EASY WAY

The story of
TED WILLIAMS
and the last .400 season

by **FRED BOWEN**

illustrations by
CHARLES S. PYLE

DUTTON CHILDREN'S BOOKS · AN IMPRINT OF PENGUIN GROUP (USA) INC.

To my brothers and sisters,
Tom, Margaret, Pete, Rich, Dave,
and Nancy. All members of the
Red Sox Nation.

F.B.

To my grandpa, Ernie, for his
love of the game, and to Tina for
encouraging me to "hit this one
out of the ballpark"

C.S.P.

Much of the information about Ted Williams and his famous 1941 season came from the books Ted Williams: A Baseball Life, by Michael Seidel, and Ted Williams: The Biography of an American Hero, by Leigh Montville.

The author thanks Jim Gates and the staff of the National Baseball Hall of Fame library for their help in researching the photographs. The author especially thanks his son, Liam Bowen, for the research he did on this project while he was a Frank and Peggy Steele intern at the National Baseball Hall of Fame and Museum.

DUTTON CHILDREN'S BOOKS
A division of Penguin Young Readers Group

Published by the Penguin Group
Penguin Group (USA) Inc., 375 Hudson Street, New York, New York 10014, U.S.A.
Penguin Group (Canada), 90 Eglinton Avenue East, Suite 700, Toronto, Ontario M4P 2Y3, Canada
    (a division of Pearson Penguin Canada Inc.)
Penguin Books Ltd, 80 Strand, London WC2R 0RL, England
Penguin Ireland, 25 St Stephen's Green, Dublin 2, Ireland (a division of Penguin Books Ltd)
Penguin Group (Australia), 250 Camberwell Road, Camberwell, Victoria 3124, Australia
    (a division of Pearson Australia Group Pty Ltd)
Penguin Books India Pvt Ltd, 11 Community Centre, Panchsheel Park, New Delhi - 110 017, India
Penguin Group (NZ), 67 Apollo Drive, Rosedale, North Shore 0632, New Zealand
    (a division of Pearson New Zealand Ltd)
Penguin Books (South Africa) (Pty) Ltd, 24 Sturdee Avenue, Rosebank, Johannesburg 2196, South Africa
Penguin Books Ltd, Registered Offices: 80 Strand, London WC2R 0RL, England

Text copyright © 2010 by Fred Bowen • Illustrations copyright © 2010 by Charles S. Pyle

IMAGES: Minneapolis AA team 1938 (p.7) and Ted Williams swing (p. 29) courtesy of National Baseball Hall of Fame library, Cooperstown, NY; Ted Williams in dugout (p.1) and Ted Williams grip (p.10) courtesy of the Associated Press.

CIP Data is available.

Published in the United States by Dutton Children's Books,
a division of Penguin Young Readers Group
345 Hudson Street, New York, New York 10014
www.penguin.com/youngreaders

Designed by Irene Vandervoort • Manufactured in China • First Edition

ISBN: 978-0-525-47877-5

10 9 8 7 6 5 4 3 2 1

Chuck S. Pyle
ILLUSTRATOR / BODY DOUBLE

The artist, **CHUCK PYLE**, dressed in a baseball uniform, bears a striking resemblance to his subject as he poses for the last picture in the book.

H itting a baseball is the single most difficult thing to do in sports."
Ted Williams said that. And Ted Williams was one of the greatest major-league hitters of all time.

Ted was tall and lean with a strong, smooth swing. With just a flick of the bat, he could hit home runs as far as anyone had ever seen. And he had an eagle eye for telling a good pitch from a bad one, so he didn't swing at bad ones.

Ted grew up in San Diego, California, in the 1930s. At that time, many people in the country were poor, and Ted's family was poorer than most. But in one way, Ted was lucky. From the time he was young, he knew exactly what he wanted to be. "My dream was to walk down the street and have people say, 'There goes Ted Williams, the greatest hitter who ever lived.'"

Some nights, sitting alone, Ted would stare into the night sky and wish upon a shooting star to be the best hitter he could be.

Ted did more than sit and wish. He played lots of baseball in the California sunshine. Ted loved to play baseball. But most of all, Ted loved to hit. He raced to school every morning so that he could be the first to hit in the schoolyard pickup games. After school, he dashed around the corner to the North Park playground so he could practice hitting.

Oh, how Ted loved to hit. He swung the bat so many times that blisters popped up like mushrooms on his hands. Then the blisters grew into hard, ugly calluses across his palms.

Ted did not mind. He knew there was no easy way to become the greatest hitter who ever lived. No easy way to do the single most difficult thing in sports: to hit a round ball with a round bat.

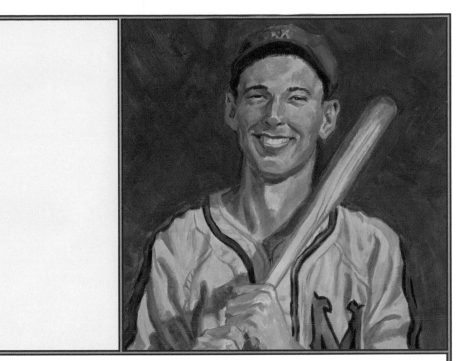

So Ted kept working . . . and practicing . . . and playing.

First at Horace Mann Junior High School . . .

then for Herbert Hoover High School . . .

then for the baseball team at the "Fighting Bob" American Legion Post . . .

then for the San Diego Padres, when they were just a minor-league team.

And then Ted moved on to another minor-league team: the Minneapolis Millers.

Finally, he was good enough for the major leagues. Ted was so excited he was almost jumping out of his skin when he arrived in Boston to play for the Red Sox. He couldn't wait to grab a bat and show everyone what a great hitter he was.

Ted showed them right away. He hit thirty-one home runs in his rookie season. Ted was so good the newspapers called him "the Kid," "the Splendid Splinter," and "Teddy Ballgame." His batting average that year was .327. Hitting over .300 in the major leagues is good.

But Ted wanted to be great. He wanted to hit .400. He knew he wouldn't get a hit every time he got up to bat—no major leaguer has ever done that. In fact, major leaguers don't even get hits half the time they're at bat. But getting a hit 40 percent of the time—batting .400—Ted thought it might be possible.

Hitting .400 would mean even more work and more practice. Just as when he was a boy, no player practiced more than Ted. "None of them hit any more balls, swung a bat in practice more than I did," he said. He swung the bat over and over until his swing was just right, strong and smooth with just a bit of an uppercut. When he wasn't batting, he squeezed rubber balls again and again to make his wrists and forearms tough and strong.

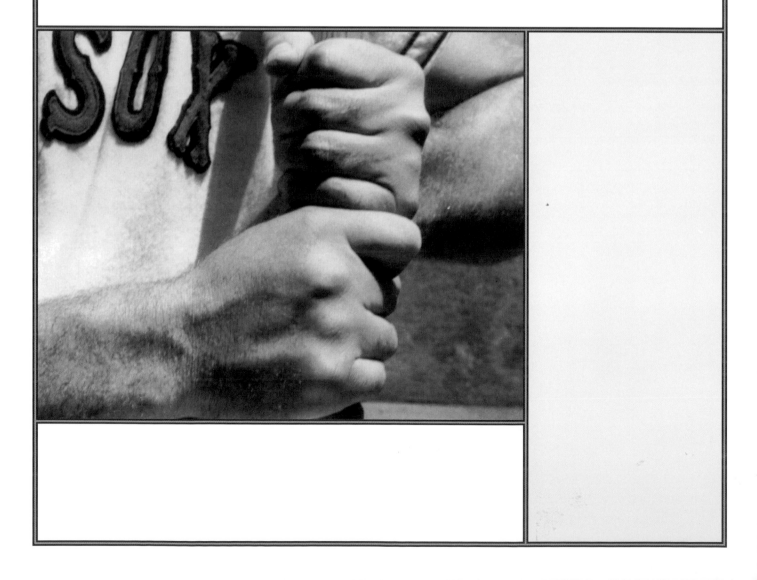

All the practice and hard work paid off two years later in 1941. That was a magic summer for baseball and for Ted Williams. It was the last summer before American soldiers went off to fight in World War II, a war so big that even the greatest baseball stars joined the military.

Stars like Hank Greenberg, the Detroit Tigers home-run champ, "Rapid Robert" Feller, the fireballing right-hander for the Cleveland Indians, and "Pee Wee" Reese, the Brooklyn Dodgers shortstop and captain. Even Joltin' Joe DiMaggio, the Yankees star center fielder, and Ted Williams went off to fight after 1941.

But that summer before the war, Joe DiMaggio was unstoppable. From May to July, he got a hit in a record-breaking fifty-six straight games.

But fifty-six games is only part of a season, not a whole season. While everyone was watching Joe DiMaggio and his amazing hitting streak, Ted Williams was hitting, too. And no one, not even Joe D, was hitting like Ted in 1941. Ted smashed hits all over American League ballparks: line shots up the middle for singles, doubles off outfield walls, and long towering drives that no ballpark could hold.

Ted's batting average took off in the cool of the spring and floated above .400 during the heat of the summer.

It rose to .436 in June.

It fell to .402 in August.

Then it went back up to .413 in September.

People started to wonder if Ted might hit .400 for the whole season. No player had done that for the longest time. And it seemed impossible that any player would ever do it again.

The promise of summer turned to the chill of autumn. Ted's batting average started to drift down, down, down, a point a day until it was at .401 with just three games to play.

Tired from the long season, Ted could only slap out a single hit in four times at bat in his next game. So now his batting average teetered on the edge at .39955. There were only two more games left in the season, a doubleheader against the Philadelphia Athletics.

But .39955 still counts as a .400 batting average. In baseball, batting averages are rounded up. So Ted had a choice. He could sit out the last two games and still be a .400 hitter in the record books. Or he could play and take the chance that he might not get enough hits to stay a .400 hitter.

The New York Yankees and the Brooklyn Dodgers were already in the World Series. Around the country, baseball fans waited for the answer to the final question of the long season: could Ted Williams do it? Could he hit .400?

The newspapers said that maybe Ted should stay on the bench for the last two games to keep his magic number. Even the Red Sox manager told Ted to sit out the Sunday doubleheader so he would not risk his chance of hitting .400.

But that would have been the easy way. And Ted knew that there was no easy way to be the greatest hitter who ever lived. No easy way to do the single most difficult thing in sports. To hit a round ball with a round bat. No easy way to be a .400 hitter.

Ted knew because that is what all his blisters and calluses and all the thousands of practice swings he had taken from North Park in San Diego until now had taught him. So Ted told his manager no thanks. "If I can't hit .400 all the way, I don't deserve it."

Ted knew the last games would not be easy. On the night before, he walked the streets of Philadelphia with his friend Johnny Orlando, who worked for the team. Ted was as nervous as a cat. The two friends walked, talked, and stopped for ice cream. Ted thought about the pitchers and the pitches he would have to face the next day. And both men wondered whether Ted could hit .400 for a season.

The last day of the season dawned cold and gray. The previous day's rain hung about the field. Still, ten thousand fans came out to see if "the Kid" could hit .400.

Ted came up to bat for the first time in the second inning. As he dug his left foot into the back of the batter's box, the Philadelphia Athletics' catcher raised his mask and said, "Ted, our manager told us that if we let up on you, he'll run us out of baseball. I wish you all the luck in the world, but we're not giving you a thing."

Then the home-plate umpire called time-out. He walked around Ted, bent over, and began dusting off the plate. Without looking up, he said, "To hit .400, a batter has got to be loose. He has got to be loose."

So Ted took a deep breath, stared out at the pitcher, and tried once again to do the single most difficult thing in sports: to hit a round ball with a round bat and to be a .400 hitter, all the way.

The first two pitches flew wide of the plate and Ted, with his eagle eye, held back.

"Get a good pitch to hit," Ted told himself. A hitter can't hit .400 swinging at bad pitches.

The next pitch was a good pitch to hit. Ted swung the bat as he had thousands of times before, smooth and strong, with just a bit of an uppercut.

Crack!

The ball rocketed into right field after ricocheting off the first baseman's mitt. Too hot to handle, the official scorer ruled. So it was a hit, a single. Ted was on his way.

Ted got up to bat again in the fifth inning. Another good pitch to hit. Another smooth, strong swing.

Crack!

This time the ball flew so far and so fast that no one could touch it. Over the right-field wall in old Shibe Park and out on to 20th Street in Philadelphia. A home run!

In the sixth inning, the Athletics brought in another pitcher, a left-hander. The Athletics' manager was keeping his promise. He wasn't going to make it easy for Ted. But it didn't matter.

Crack!

Ted smacked a line drive right up the middle for another single.

In the eighth inning—

Crack!

A hot smash down the right-field line. Another hit.

Ted finished the game with four hits in five times at bat. His batting average rose to .404.

Now would Ted sit down for the second game to save his record?

No way! If Ted was going to hit .400, he was going to do it all the way.

So Ted played. He knocked out two more hits in three turns at bat. He smashed a line drive off a loudspeaker in right field for a double. He hit it so hard that the Athletics had to get a new loudspeaker.

And Ted's batting average rose to .406.

That is so much better than .39955.

.406.

That's now one of the most famous numbers in baseball. Because it's the batting average of the last player in the major leagues to hit .400 for a whole season. It's the batting average of the last player to hit .400 all the way. . . . Ted Williams.

There was no easy way, but Ted Williams did it.

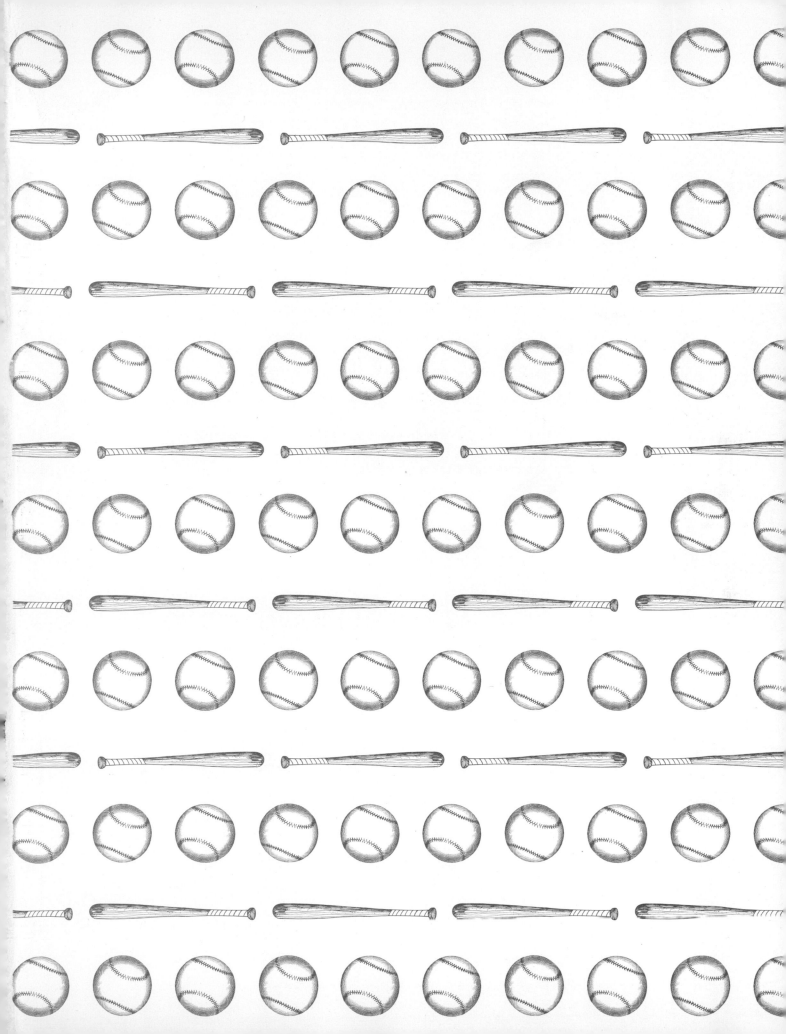

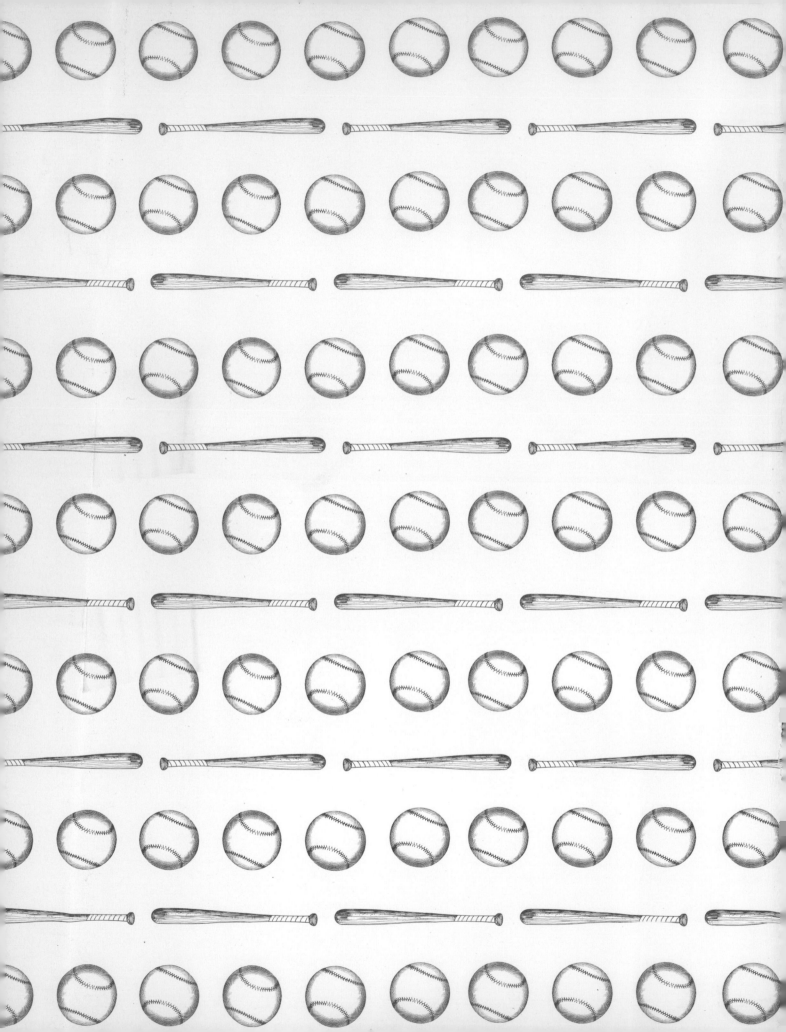